DAMAGED

BY ADULT ADD

STEPS TOWARD WHOLENESS FOR YOURSELF AND YOUR FAMILY

BY

RON WOOD

FOREWORD

During my psychiatric training at Johns Hopkins Hospital, I was taught that Attention Deficit Disorder was a diagnosis limited to children and adolescence. During my 35 years of clinical practice, both the field of psychiatry and myself have discovered that up to 50% of ADD children and adolescents continue to have attention deficit problems into adulthood. My oldest patient is now 81 years old. I recommend Rev. Wood's <u>Damaged by Adult ADD</u> *as an extremely helpful guide especially for adults with this disorder.*

Daniel Y. Patterson, MD, MPH
Wilmington, NC

As Solomon said in the Scriptures, "There is nothing new under the sun." Indeed, this is the case with adult attention deficit disorder (ADD). Prior to our recognition of this as a legitimate diagnosis in adults, people did their best to cope with it with, results varying from truly impressive to tragic. Utilizing his unique gift of communication, Pastor Ron Wood provides us in this writing with a practical guide to help us address this complex disorder.

J. Michael Nanney, MD
Primary Care Associates, Meridian, MS

HOW ADD AFFECTS YOUR MARRIAGE AND CAREER

FOR YEARS I WONDERED why walking through a busy shopping mall was unpleasant and disorienting. There was too much visual stimulation. Too much input felt overwhelming. It made me feel uneasy, almost nauseous, like I had mild motion sickness. I thought everyone was like this except that I had poorer self-control.

So, I would walk through a busy shopping mall with my eyes cast down. I tried to avoid scanning all the attractive images and pretty colors. That way, I could keep my mind focused on why I was there and remember to search only for what I had come to purchase. This was a feature of my life until I was fifty years old.

In elementary school, if my seat was in the back of the class, I was out of luck. With a last name near the end of the alphabet, that happened a lot. The visual sea of moving, murmuring, wiggling, noisy students within my field of vision was like a waving curtain between me and the teacher or the chalkboard. It was hopelessly distracting.

Fortunately, I was soon diagnosed as being nearsighted. Because of my condition, the teachers began to keep me closer to the front so I could see better until I got glasses. This was an accidental blessing. From the front row, I could pay attention much easier. I needed to be in the front row so I could learn and not be distracted. My Attention Deficit Disorder was moderated.

Now that I'm an older adult, I have served as a substitute teacher in several public and private schools. I can readily see the harm that undiagnosed ADD is causing many younger students. Bright boys and girls (more boys are often afflicted than girls) begin to suffer with poor grades. Often due to ADD — let alone childish immaturity — they lack the ability to be still, to focus or to finish tasks. Or they become overwhelmed with too much input and can't filter out the signal from the noise. This takes a real toll on their grades. If it is ADD or ADHD, their poor grades have very little to do with their intelligence. Nor does frequently misbehaving mean they are not respecting their teacher, at least not on purpose. They are not dumb. They are not bad kids. They are not rebels. They don't deserve to be punished. They simply may suffer from undiagnosed or untreated ADD.

With ADD in children, associated behavioral issues may show up. To the parents, the signs seem to point to bad character, willful rebellion, or disrespect toward the teacher. They think their child is not listening. But the issue is possibly something they are not able to control without help just like I couldn't read the writing on the chalkboard unless I moved closer or could put on corrective eyeglasses.

Can you imagine the harm that this disability causes to a child, to his or her identity? It can affect their confidence. It begins to affect their perception of their self as a competent human able to learn. Self-esteem and confidence in their ability begins to plummet. They start to see themselves as a failure.

For me, as a child and as a teenager, I loved to learn. I had been gifted with a brilliant mind. I was able to learn quickly and had excellent comprehension. In a classroom environment, I could thrive because I was curious and able to hyper-focus. I learned how to memorize answers. Many ADDers can do this. I'll say more on this topic later. I could make an "A" on any test that I chose to study for *if* I was interested. But if I was bored? The necessary stimulus to pay attention wasn't there.

School was usually interesting though. Later, I caught a wave of advanced classes in both junior and senior high right after Russia launched Sputnik and America worked hard to catch up. I had Advanced Math, Geometry, Trigonometry, English, Speech, Chemistry, Biology, Science, and Physics. I even had four years of Latin. I was fortunate in that I received one of the best public school educations offered.

Looking back, ADD was not a minor thing. All through my life the fact of ADD – even though no one knew about it or called it by that name back then – was always with me, always plaguing me and in a peculiar way, blessing me. But the problems being caused by ADD increased as I grew older.

When I first began to earn a living, I had to be careful with any work that required monitoring a lot of details. I could multi-task given the opportunity to learn, but it required focus. For instance, my job at a radio station required complex interactions with the control board and minute by minute awareness of the clock. Each hour was unique and things changed quickly. Other than playing the sign-off anthem at 3 o'clock in the afternoon, I eventually did well. The time on my four-hour on-air shift flew by. The station owner appreciated me. He wanted to train me to become of his station managers but I declined.

When a friend challenged me to play a game of backgammon, I tried but at first it was impossible for me to comprehend. But I kept at it, repeatedly failing, frustrated, until finally, something clicked. I saw it! I rarely lost again. The same with Chinese checkers.

Another area I noticed my deficit was meeting new people in large numbers. In my role as a pastor (my primary career), I was required to meet new people frequently. I was expected to know their names after the first introduction. For me, this was very challenging since busy settings and multiple new faces didn't give me the chance to lock in on their identity. So, I would avoid contact with folks if their name eluded me. This was embarrassing. Not good. I like people and have good social skills, but this was interfering with my work. At that time, I didn't have a clue why I felt this way or had this difficulty.

When I became married, the inability to handle multiple items without being distracted caused me to begin doubting myself. Frustrations due to being distracted or dropping the ball began to affect my marriage. A biggie? I would forget to pay a bill! Anger began to invade my self-talk but I couldn't identify the cause.

Twenty years into starting my marriage, with a loving wife and two delightful kids, I realized I had *all of the symptoms* of Adult ADD—*all of them!*

I sighed with relief when I figured it out. I learned about my own ADD by watching my two bright children struggle in high school. Both were diagnosed with some degree of ADD. Thank God, both are now successful adults in their careers and marriages and are truly remarkable human beings.

I joked about my discovery and said, "I caught ADD from my kids!" But ADD is no joke, I assure you. This book is my story. This is what I learned. I wish I had known it sooner. I'm sharing my story so you won't go through the same struggles as me.

But first, what is ADD? What do I need to know? How can I recognize it? What can I do about it?

ADD AFFECTS ADULTS

ADD IS A DISABILITY. The word comes from the abbreviation for Attention Deficit Disorder. It may have the component of Hyper-Activity Disorder in children and then it's usually called ADHD.

Some medical scholars wonder if ADD may be on the autism spectrum. I won't speculate. Others think it is simply a different wiring in the brain; a peculiar way of paying attention (or not) that some kids might outgrow. What makes sense to me is the discovery that ADD-afflicted folks have a part of their brain that filters out less-important data so the brain can work on important things.

There has been controversy about its diagnosis and its treatment. This is because the usual or original treatment for school children was Ritalin, a prescription drug that stimulates certain portions of the brain thus making the part of it that monitors outside stimulus work better. With medical help, children or adults can filter out distractions easier. This helps to control restlessness and impulsivity. The drug treatment works in both adults and children in a similar way. Other types of ADD medications are available now. More are coming to the market.

Children with ADHD have shown dramatic improvement in their education when properly diagnosed and treated. It is generally the over-use of prescriptions or reactions to the idea of the drug itself (a controlled substance) that causes the controversy. Parents dislike the idea that their child needs a prescription. Only a trained doctor can tell for sure.

Prescriptions that benefit adults with ADD are similar in their effect. The drugs make part of the brain more alert. Once that area of the brain wakes up, it can do what it was designed to do. Many respected, successful people use ADD medication. You wouldn't know it by observing them, except that they can function much better when they are on their meds, without any long-term harm to their body.

While the struggles of children with ADD or ADHD are prominent, it is not so common for us to discuss the struggles of adults. The consequences of ignorance about Adult ADD can be very serious.

Dawn McMullen is the author of the article, "Living with Adult ADD," in D Magazine. It was published in their special "Dallas Medical Directory" in 2009 and is available online. She wrote,

"Never has our society been more focused on an issue that just 20 years ago was incredibly misunderstood by doctors, parents, teachers—just about everyone. The bad news is, about 5 percent of adults have attention deficit disorder (ADD) or its constantly moving cousin, attention deficit hyperactivity disorder (ADHD). For them, the learning curve is steep. They carry baggage from damaged self-esteem. Adults with ADD are more likely to drop out of college, get fired from jobs, abuse drugs and alcohol, and divorce."

In her article, McMullen describes a man who "...followed a fairly predictable path of someone who doesn't deal with his ADD. He used alcohol and drugs—illegal and prescribed—to self-medicate. Jobs usually didn't last more than a few years because they got boring or stressful, just like college did. Relationships were often unstable."

She noted another cause—the ADDer's brain craves stimulation, often in the form of drama. She went on to say...

"Many ADD adults have tried self-medicating with alcohol and drugs. Some people call it an addictive personality. Dr. David Clark, a chiropractic neurologist in Dallas, sees it as a brain that does not have the machinery to keep an even keel. Dr. Clark said, *'The vast majority of people who have these problems are prone to various types of addictions, be it illegal or otherwise.'*"

Her article described some people whose lives went out of control and spiraled down into chaos. My response is to give you this analogy of a car with bad brakes.

Untreated ADD in adults is like driving a car at a very fast pace, a car that you know has bad brakes. Eventually, you will have a wreck. Eventually, the people you love will be hurt. Eventually, you'll suffer losses that could've been avoided.

So why not take an ounce of prevention to prevent a pound of pain?

KNOW YOURSELF

MY PERSPECTIVE on this subject comes from two viewpoints: seeing my own children (who are now successful adults) struggle with ADD and by observation, discovering I had it also. Then with years of experience and a lot of thought, fitting this problem into my own understanding of what it means to live as a Christian adult, otherwise responsible and capable, but with shortcomings.

Now I know how to accept my disability. I can cope with it. To a certain degree, I can even overcome it. My realism includes self-acceptance and a plan. My plan is more than medications; it incorporates an understanding of how life works. It includes my spouse's active role. I've gained this viewpoint of acceptance plus pro-active self-care based on many years of work as a pastor.

In my career in churches I talked with and helped a lot of people so they could overcome their personal challenges, their addictions, bad habits, and damaged marriages. Life is tough enough without first dealing with your internal issues like ADD or depression.

Of course, most (but not all) adult personal pain is self-inflicted. It is due to sin and the consequences of our bad choices or individual foolishness. We can't blame irresponsibility or self-deception about how life works on our ADD. This may be old fashioned for me to say, but sin makes people stupid!

If we could live by righteous standards, applying godly wisdom, life would be so much better ADD or not. I've made the statement that I would follow Jesus and live in His kingdom even if there were no heaven or no hell, simply because it's the best and most satisfying way to live on earth.

The ideas I will share about Adult ADD and its effects on your family can be genuine lifesavers. Some of these insights are original to me. Many ideas come from my sources, from the random notes I wrote to help myself as I read articles online plus the books that I will list. A lot of helpful ideas are digested here for you. My intent is to credit the ideas and terms to the writers who helped me when I learned I had ADD. But the perspective I present is uniquely mine. The research and advice comes from various sources.

This book will let you look over my shoulder as I learned how to handle this ailment. It has been a painful journey for me but worth the effort. You will benefit greatly by not having to make the same mistakes I made. I've included a list of excellent authors that I quote or reference, plus some other books we suggest. I hope you can utilize them.

This story is taken from my own life experience. It is personal and practical. However, this material is not intended as medical advice. This is for informational use only. It is a testimonial of what I dealt with and learned about myself. It should not and cannot replace your own consultation with a qualified physician. I am not a physician. I'm just a man with true story, one told by a father and husband who happens to be an author and a minister.

I have some informed opinions that I am offering here. My insights are educational and inspirational, aimed at guiding you along the path of your own self-discovery. These are self-improvement steps toward greater personal happiness and a much-improved family life. They can make a big difference for you.

Why is this information important? Almost everyone knows someone with ADD. Maybe you have ADD. But do you know this? Undiagnosed Adult ADD can be devastating to you, damaging to your family, and disastrous to your career. It can literally wreck your life. Adult ADD has cost people their marriages, their jobs, and their emotional health. Your own family may already be suffering due to untreated ADD.

Here is another important fact: Undiagnosed ADD in children will cause years of frustration, poor grades, slow advancement, and may even cause the child to give up on school or worse; to give up on themselves. They may believe that they are a failure, or that they are stupid. You don't want that for your child!

ADD is not something you can treat or get over without help. Usually, you can't outgrow it either; at least for about one-third of those who have it as a child. These issues are among the reasons why I wrote this little book—first for me but also for you.

Gather the information you need and then get the treatment you or your loved ones deserve. Don't live in denial. There is no shame in having ADD. You didn't ask for it. You were born with it. But there is shame in knowing you have it but not facing it honestly or seeking medical care. That's why this book was written; to uncover hidden ADD. It might help you or someone you love. Knowing yourself is essential.

Some of the issues I faced in my life, when they were corrected, resulted in wonderful improvements in my marriage, my work skills, and especially in my own self-image. Ask my wife—she will quickly tell that you she is glad we obtained competent counseling and skilled medical assistance. If only I had known what I needed to do earlier as a man. I'm sure that a lot of grief could have been avoided.

I learned that I had to take responsibility for my own recovery. What's my part in getting better? Is there something I can do differently? Is there someone I need to forgive—including myself? What part of my life is out of balance?

We all—especially ADD adults living in the fast lane of life—tend to live without sufficient reflection. ADDers are poor self-observers. People with ADD often do not have a very accurate perception of their own self.

We can't see ourselves objectively so we don't know ourselves very well. Sometimes for me, I don't even know when I am hungry. That is, until I smell the aroma or sit down in front of the delicious food my wife prepared.

Some of these stories might be like a mirror that is held up to reflect you. Can you see yourself on these pages? Maybe you will before you finish reading. You might see someone you love or care about. Do you suspect that this is what they need? This information may cause you or your loved one to consult a physician, just to be sure.

Is life a blur of activity with little significance or satisfaction? We can't substitute *doing* for *being*. Busy-ness is not satisfying. That's self-deception, like a hamster racing on an exercise wheel. I am defined by who I am, not by what I do. I'm a *human being* not a *human doing*.

Whatever I may attempt in life always goes much better if I first become centered, more self-aware, and able to move out from a place of peace to accomplish a task. Since realizing my own situation I can now be more *present to the moment.* I understand myself. This is such a delightful zone to enter. I can enjoy being me!

A HOLISTIC APPROACH

WE SHOULD ALL be on a journey toward more wholeness in body, soul, and spirit. With our body, we relate to the material world. With our soul, we relate to other people. With our spirit, we relate to God. Each part of us needs to be alive and functioning. If not, we remain incomplete individuals and to a degree, we remain fragmented. The parts don't work well together. Who wants to be a voluntary cripple? Who wants to have some part of their life that is always out of balance? Don't settle!

The first step toward being whole and happy is to make up your mind that this new path is your desire. You have the power of choice. Reject more of the past as unacceptable. Choose to learn, grow, and overcome. You can do this. You can make an informed decision to bring your struggles into the light. Set your mind and heart toward becoming a more whole human being.

Wholeness means being healthy and happy. It is the opposite of *dis*order (not in order) or *dis*ease (not having ease). Wholeness has to do with the whole person being fully integrated, fully functional, without schism or divisions, nothing hidden or ailing in their personality.

Wholeness is a state of being well, a mature integration of the entire self, not being fragmented. Let's look at another way of seeing this wholeness. Consider the word, integrated. The root of this word is *integrity*. In ordinary language if we say, "That person has integrity," we are giving them a compliment. We are saying, "They are not a hypocrite," meaning we see them as being truthful, not two-faced, not a pretender. What you see is what you get. They are who they say they are, through and through. There is nothing concealed or dishonest, but they are authentic and genuine all the time.

A person who has integrity has a soul that is integrated. Body, mind, and soul are one, not splintered. Their mind is clear and coherent. They are not double-minded, not doubting their own self or dismissing their dreams. They have unified their beliefs, emotions, and choices.

How can we stop being at war with our self and instead be united in our soul? Begin with knowing how you are made. Our self as a person has three parts: *physical, psychological, and spiritual.* Did you know this about yourself?

From the New Testament, the Bible gives us insight about this. In the original language, it uses three different Greek words to describe these three distinct aspects of our human life.

From the Old Testament, the Hebrew understanding of creation is that these aspects unify to make us into a whole human being. Body and soul are one being.

I like this biblical insight since it fits what we know of science and psychology. It rings true as I observe people. As a pastor and Bible teacher, I have a high regard for biblical insight and revelation.

In Greek, the *body* is **soma**. The *soul* is **psuche**. The *spirit* is **pneuma**. This reference can be found in the Bible in First Thessalonians chapter 5, verse 23, in the New Testament.

Why is this important to understand? The reason is that we need to be able to diagnose our own invisible internal pains and sicknesses. Not all disabilities are physical. Not all pain is located in the body. Emotional pain is also very real. Trauma can be mental. It needs to be healed.

Here is another way to look at these vital but distinct parts of our being. With our *body*, we experience pain or pleasure. With our *soul*, we experience happiness or sadness. With our *spirit*, we experience joy or grief.

Our human body allows us to interact with material things in this world. Our human soul allows us to interact with other people. And with our spirit we can interact with God, the Father of our spirit.

We were created to experience life and enjoy it fully in all three of these dimensions - spirit, soul, and body. Wholeness in these three areas allows us to experience happiness and joy.

If one part of our human self is not well or is dysfunctional, it affects the other parts of us. The mind-body connection is real. The technical word used by physicians is *psychosomatic,* a combination of two Greek words, for soul and body. That is why an emotional wound, if left unresolved, can cause your physical body to become ill. It can also cause you to habitually make bad choices, to try to self-medicate. A symptom of having an emotional wound from a childhood trauma or a broken relationship could be an irrational feeling like fear, anger, or resentment. This can make you sick in your soul and eventually affect your body.

Imbedded memories of emotional trauma are real and don't necessarily go away with time. They need to be resolved. Likewise, chronic pain in the body can certainly affect your state of mind or impact your feelings. This is also true of our innermost part, our spirit (the inner person of the heart). Is your spirit lively? Or is it depressed, rejected, sick with rejection, hurt, or bitterness? I am glad there is a real cure for all of these invisible wounds. The cure can be physical, mental, or spiritual.

We can and should be healthy both inside and outside. We can be free to love and be loved again.

Wholeness includes freedom from addictions, healthy attitudes, good emotions, physical fitness, right thinking, and the ability to relate to others with integrity so that you will never be a victim. That means being able to uphold healthy boundaries to protect yourself from dysfunctional people.

Being whole includes loving yourself properly. Hating yourself is not normal. By right thinking, I mean true thoughts that are clear and positive. The balance to be able to live well is best achieved by an acceptance of your self — a state of peace that ultimately proceeds from knowing God's view of you. People suffering with significant ADD often lack true peace of mind.

"It is not those who are healthy who need a physician, but those who are sick," Jesus, the physician of our soul, said these words in Matthew 9:12. He said this to urge compassion, not criticism.

All of us suffer from some type of disorder that needs curing, whether by medicine, counseling, lifestyle adjustments, repentance, or by the power of divine grace. Many ailments are invisible to others, at least initially, but we all have them.

All of us have some disease that needs to be brought to peace. Remember, "dis-ease" means the absence of ease, the lack of rest, or to be robbed of peace. Rather than judge those who are ill or bound or weak, let's show mercy. Let's find out how to help ourselves first and then help our friends and loved ones along the way.

Let's start the journey of discovery about ADD and learn how it impacts our life or our family. To do this, there are things you need to know.

HUNTER OR FARMER?

TOM HARTMANN is a writer who has led thousands of hours of discussion groups concerning ADD in online forums. In his book, *Think Fast, Tom* says the human race is divided into two camps: Hunters and Farmers.

In this helpful word picture, the hunters (I imagine hungry lions slinking through tall grass) are constantly monitoring every movement, hyper-attentive, and are capable of short bursts of incredible energy. The farmers (I picture men leaning on a fence watching their cattle) move steadily and walk slowly and plow straight lines and wait for the grain to grow and for the seasons to change. What a powerful analogy!

The hunters live among the farmers. The hunters are people with ADD while the farmers represent normal people. They see each other, but they often don't understand each other. They have trouble communicating, like a Mac computer trying to talk to a PC. Which kind of person are you? Are you a hunter or are you a farmer? Let's find out. What's it like to have ADD?

Well, life is never dull, that's for sure. Have you ever walked into a room searching for something only to forget what you came looking for? I have. Have you ever started to take out the garbage as your wife requested, only to see the checkbook lying on the table, start to pay the bills, realize you needed to update your software, wind up being late to work, and still forget to take out the garbage? Yep, I've done it. Do you always carry a book with you so you won't be bored? I always do! Do you write notes to yourself then lose the notes? Oh yeah, done that.

If you always have your checkbook balanced, if you are able to sit still in a chair, if you never speak out of turn, then you don't know what it's like to have ADD. (I am so glad my wife does *not* have ADD!)

A Psychotherapist MD (who has ADD) says this: "It is like driving in a hard rain with bad windshield wipers, constantly straining to see clearly." Isn't that a vivid description? Can you picture what that's like? He goes on to say, "You get an idea and you have to act on it immediately, before you lose it. Your head is buzzing, spinning, and your body is tapping, moving." He also says, "The definition of time is, 'the thing that keeps everything from happening at once.' With ADD, time collapses."

To me, time seems to always collapse in my world. I'm often totally lost or unaware of the passage of time.

The doctor goes on to say, "You fight inner turmoil, panic, loss of control. Your brain rhythm is either full speed ahead, or full stop, with no in between. You have a constant quest for stimulation for your mind but you have to withdraw from people due to over-stimulation. You are always either under-focused or over-focused. Either your body or your mind is racing all the time." This description is insightful and on target.

Knowing this, perhaps you can see why to someone with ADD, *boredom is painful.* The structured American public school classroom, often moving at the snail's pace of the slowest child, feels like a prison, like a torture trap to be escaped from at all cost. Most untreated ADD kids don't do well in school.

While too much rigid structure seems like a cage, *some structure* is exactly what ADD adults need to harness their creativity, reduce distractions, and stay on track to complete projects.

I found out that I had ADD by observing my kids. That's when my lightbulb went on.

For me, the discovery that I had ADD was a relief. My years of self-recrimination and frustration for dropping important dates, forgetting things, losing track of figures, getting lost in a task, putting trivial things at the same priority as urgent tasks, searching for my keys only to find them in my hand, etc., etc., came to an end. Well, at least the awful silent self-accusations ended.

Understanding ADD was very beneficial to me personally. I could forgive myself. I could even laugh at myself, which is important. I could accept that I had a handicap, albeit an invisible one. At least now I could identify it as an attribute, like being tall or short or near-sighted, and I could learn to cope with it in a realistic way. ADD is always unique to each individual, with some common features, but varying degrees of affliction.

My major symptoms were three-fold: *easy distractibility*, especially visually stimulating things like TV; *crowded thinking,* with floods of thoughts rushing in simultaneously; and what I call *compacted time*, where clocks and calendars are a blur and everything seems to happen concurrently with no sequence or space in between.

No one can become more lost in time while writing or editing than me. When I'm writing, I'll almost always lose track of any sense of time. Hours will pass and I'll discover that I've been sitting without moving for six straight hours.

That is actually an asset to me since I can accomplish a great deal and I genuinely love writing. But it is also a liability. Therefore, I use reminders or alarms on my phone so I can remember to move on to the next appointment or to the next task.

I have trained myself to be more self-aware and I've been treated for my ADD. I can usually recognize it when I'm slipping into areas where I have a weakness. My boundaries are more recognizable or distinct so I can put up a guard against exceeding my limits. I can better spot my own feelings or my loss of focus. I can catch areas that are vulnerable due to fatigue, mental strain, missing a meal, or the lack of exercise. For example, I have learned: *never* attempt to balance a checkbook late in the day!

In the event my behavior needs deliberate, conscious adjustment, my wife knows to speak up and remind me. I've learned not to react negatively to this, nor to get angry with her for helping me. I need her! In our family, she is the only one who is a straight-line thinker. Calling attention to my ADD behavior is one way that she serves me, by having the love and the liberty to say something to me.

I am sorry to confess this, but before my diagnosis, I felt — wrongly and irrationally — that she was correcting me; like she was judging me for something that I could not fix. Back then, I took her helpful comments as though she was rejecting me or putting me down. I made it hard for her. All she was doing was telling me the truth in love, trying to be of help.

Before I realized that I was struggling with ADD, I was often angry, defensive and impatient with her or with frustrating situations. I needed help!

Here is an interesting way that my ADD affects me. Numbers don't communicate to me like words do, even when I'm at my best. Words are fluent, marvels of revelation; sparkling gems of communication while numbers remain a maddening mystery. Numbers lie to me! I like the symmetry of math, the order, but the figures seem elusive; too tiny to mentally grip for very long.

I truly appreciate those around me who are skilled at math or accounting. However, I have learned that practice makes perfect. Our brains are more pliable than scientists used to think. We can literally grow new neural pathways with repetition, in order to learn new things. So I play Sudoku and have a lot more confidence with numbers. But, my wife keeps the books.

I have found that putting things on paper in a visual form greatly aids my comprehension of numbers - whether handling finances or budgeting time for a project. Then of course, I have the challenge of handling the paper I have produced. For ADD-afflicted people like me, it can become a flurry of drifting white stuff spilling over the edges of my desk.

I discovered after years of sweating bullets over financial issues that my wife loves to handle our family bookkeeping. And she's good at it. We have family budget meetings as needed and we tackle issues as a team, but she competently handles all the details. Life works so much better now!

She is a marvelous administrator and organizer. I think she'd make a terrific "Love Boat" cruise director in charge of all the shipboard entertainment. She'd also make a topnotch CEO of a complex business enterprise. Her ability to stay on top of details causes anyone who knows her to respect and admire her abilities. Me? I am not able to do that.

But operating as a unique husband-wife team with very different gifts, we are amazing!

DENIAL AND ADULT ADD

IF YOU DISCOVER you have A.D.D. (or suspect it has you) there are usually several stages you will go through as you learn more about yourself. These stages are similar to the well-known Kubler-Ross model for the stages of grief, which are:

Denial. "This can't be happening to me!"

Anger. "I don't deserve this!" This is usually self-directed, an inward slow boil that other people have difficulty understanding. For me, this was a *big* issue. In my life, it was a secret habit that the Lord confronted me over. I had to confess it and renounce it like any other sin. I learned to forgive myself and to stop my constant interior self-criticism. As a result I obtained forgiveness, deliverance, self-acceptance, and lasting peace.

Bargaining. "If I take my medications, the problem will go away." No. ADD won't ever completely go away. You will cope with it every day.

Depression. "Depression is a serious (and common) problem for people with ADD," says Susan Roberts. Depression is frequently misdiagnosed or goes unnoticed in people with ADD. It is often overlooked as a component of ADD thus making life even more difficult for the sufferer and for their family. Tell your doctor!

Acceptance. You decide you will take your meds and cope, just like people wear glasses to correct their vision. You learn to love yourself.

ADD has been described medically as a disorder, but with "positive attachments." That was a new thought for me. What can be positive about it? ADDers are usually very creative, highly intuitive, and usually intelligent. Many creative writers or artists have ADD. Talented visionaries with ADD are typically Global Thinkers. They can envision big concepts or hold a high perspective or absorb a lot of information at once, but they are not able to juggle all the little details to make it happen. They can think creatively "outside the box" and they can intuitively leap to correct conclusions that logical thinkers have no way of understanding.

When they are included as part of a team that appreciates their value and understands their limitations, they can move from being simply unique to being extraordinarily gifted. But they must know their limitations and they must be celebrated as part of the team.

The following statement by Dr. Whiteman is important to know.

"Sustained attention is expensive for an ADDer," says Thomas Whiteman, PhD, in his book, Adult ADD. *"The mental energy expended is enormous and taxing."* Brain fog is real. The brain is your body's largest consumer of energy in your body. Yes, thinking is hard work!

One thing about intense concentration for ADDers may surprise you. If a person with ADD can somehow create or find an environment where there are no distractions, they may be able to "hyper-focus" very intensely for sustained periods of time. It still consumes a great deal of mental energy but it can produce powerful results when an adult is on a deadline, writing, researching, doing artwork, etc. Their brain is working very hard to pull together many disconnected thoughts, ideas, and images and collate them into a new coherent whole.

As a boy, I discovered that if I turned off all the room lights except for one small desk lamp on my desk that my father gave me, I could get lost for several hours working quietly on my stamp collection, sorting the colorful stamps and placing them into my album. But if I was in the den reading intently, and anyone called my name, I would not hear it. I was hyper-focused! If you walked up behind me and touched my back, I would jump like a scalded cat. A strong startle reflex is often part of this package deal.

Fortunately, as a healthy boy who loved the outdoors, I could follow up these hyper-focused study times with activities that involved lots of physical play and exercise. Time to recoup emotional and mental energy is important for people with ADD.

Let me illustrate how ADD involves a struggle. I had the good fortune this year to serve as a substitute teacher in some public schools as well as in one private school. This is something I do part-time. I'm intrigued with how we learn new things. How do we educate? How do we teach? What are we doing wrong? What are we doing right? My friend, Rex Miller, just published his book about humanizing the education model. But I want to point out something that I learned this year from a disabled child.

The most insightful season for me this year came when I worked with an accomplished first grade teacher for six weeks. I watched her routine and her techniques. I saw how the children learned and how their progress was measured. But the highest insight came from the special needs child in her room that I was serving.

This child was afflicted with cerebral palsy. To get around, he had to use a walker with wheels, or he had to make his legs move using the special short walking canes just his size, with three prongs with rubber tips. I shadowed him all day long at school for six weeks. I greeted him in the morning behind the school when he was carried off the school bus and handed to me. I helped him inside his first-grade classroom as he moved to the different learning stations. I helped him transition into his seat at the table or on to the carpet for story time or get to the door to use his walker for a trip down the hall to a different room. I helped him to use to the toilet. I helped strap him into the special device designed to strengthen his legs. I helped him head to the office at the end of the school day when his father or mother picked him up. To me, this child was a hero. He was the epitome of courage.

I walked with him around that huge school three to four miles *every day*; up and down through the wide corridors, to the lunch room and the playground and the gym and his classroom and to therapy. If you watched him, you would not know how many times he had to stop and take a break, and say, "Could you push me, Mr. Ron?" I would say, "No, you can do this!"

He had to expend ten times the energy of any normal child just to get from point A to point B. Yet he never complained, never felt sorry for himself, never tried to skip the hard work. He always had a smile and always kept going, even when he got blisters on his feet inside his special shoes. If you looked up the word "perseverance" in the dictionary, his picture is posted with the definition. I admired him.

Why am I telling you this story? Because for me with ADD, and for thousands of other adults, we identify with the extra effort this young child exerted. For any of us with ADD — the effort to stay on track, to avoid distractions, to not fall short of completing a project, to make ourselves go all the way to the end of the journey — requires the same mental effort, stamina, exertion, and self-discipline as that brave and beautiful boy living with his obvious disability.

Besides this mental fatigue, ADDers fight forgetfulness all the time. They often have severe self-recrimination for their inability to stay focused. They forget important dates and events. Failure in relationships makes them retreat from emotional intimacy. They often deceive themselves and pretend they have no problem and sometimes lash out.

Anger is a common problem due to frequent battles with frustration. ADDers can be accused of being self-absorbed. It is because they are trying so hard to focus. They often have a poor self-image. Their anger is usually aimed internally. "If only I tried harder," they may say. They often have a running internal dialogue of habitual self-criticism. Constant self-criticism is not a good characteristic. It is not part of a wholesome self-image. Nor is it a type of healthy humility. Being mad at yourself frequently is just a bad habit. Stop doing it! It won't help the situation at all.

Having ADD is not a moral shortcoming. Did you hear me? You are not to blame. You are not a bad person. *You are not at fault but you are still responsible.* It is a condition at birth of unknown origin. It is a certain way that a person's brain is wired from childhood. ADD is a permanent situation that can be moderated but not eliminated. Do not condemn yourself. Cope? Yes! Condemn? No!

NOTE - The three preceding paragraphs are so important that you might want to take time to go back and slowly re-read them. Go ahead... I'll wait for you!

Here is a checklist that I have compiled from my reading that helps identify people who might suffer from ADD. Realize that not all symptoms will apply to everyone, and understand that some symptoms can get better with self-awareness, medical treatment, relationship counseling, and by training yourself to practice coping skills.

Mysteriously, some symptoms may abate as we age. While the medical research may still be out on this area, it is *my opinion* that ADD is not related to Alzheimer's disease, senility, or dementia. More study about this is needed.

SEE YOUR SYMPTOMS

SEE IF THE things I describe in this list are occurring regularly in your life. Do they seem to apply to you? Are they common? Are any of these things spoken about you by those who know you the best? Check for yourself on this list:

Do things impulsively

Always on the go, restless

Need help handling emotions

Always fighting frustrations

Need to build your self-image

Hard to control your temper

A substance abuser

Unable to organize a schedule

Can't prioritize to do important things first

Have trouble managing finances

Start things but don't finish them

Difficulty with time or following through

Forget things easily

Lose or misplace things often

Difficulty in school or classes

Trouble communicating your feelings

Not a good listener, always interrupting

Relationships in crisis, constant turmoil

Easily distracted; can't focus for long

The characteristic of not listening attentively before speaking was a BIG challenge for me. I could and often did finish the sentences of others while they were speaking to me. Or, I would give my reply before they were done talking.

That wasn't very smart of me. It came across to them like I presumed to know exactly what they were going to say. It felt to them like I was a "know it all" or a "smart-aleck" who didn't want to hear their thoughts, opinions, or ideas. That wasn't true. But my mind simply worked so fast that my mouth would engage and speak before I stopped it. It was so rude!

I have learned to better control that impulsivity— although not always, nor perfectly, and sometimes, *nada*.

The thoughts in my mind flow fast. That trait is still seen in my handwriting. It is quite messy. I frequently get comments like, "Your handwriting or your signature looks like a doctor's." I reply, "When I was young, I wanted to be a doctor but God called me to preach. Now I'm a soul-doctor!" My handwriting looks like hieroglyphics because my mind works faster than my pen can write. I can't read my own writing after 24 hours. I was delighted when I discovered the joy of computers. Using writing software is as much fun to me as an adult as was riding a bicycle when I was a child. I can now type nearly as fast as I can think, although with typos.

Is ADD in adults just an excuse? No, it is a real medical condition. Medically, ADD-afflicted individuals have been termed "minimally brain damaged." It appears first in childhood, often with hyperactivity, and usually persists into adulthood to some degree. Dr. Ratep wrote, *"ADD is a problem of the frontal lobes (of the brain) where information is sorted out and acted upon."* He calls ADD, *"An impairment."*

Today neurological researchers, especially the pioneering medical research by Dr. Daniel Amen, can electronically map the unusual electrical patterns of our brains as they function in distinct ADD styles. It is not an imagined condition, but it is a measurable physiological phenomenon. It can be viewed on digital images of the brain.

While several types of ADD have been identified, three major areas are categorized socially but not scientifically by one insightful counselor and writer who herself has ADD. These three adaptive personality styles are:

The Active Entertainer - Expressive, outgoing, a risk-taker, a salesman. He or she rolls the dice but forgets that it may cost them dearly. Enjoyable to work with but needs task-orientation tools.

The Restless Dreamer - Fights frustration. Often inwardly focused. This kind of ADD person is often misdiagnosed. They may battle severe depression due to stuffing their real feelings. The Restless Dreamer needs appreciation and encouragement and must listen and accept realistic goals. These first two ADD personality types need some personalized structure in order to succeed.

The Conscientious Controller - compensates by extreme control, rigid rituals, and excessive structure, or requiring constant perfectionism. He makes a good accountant, but may be difficult to live with.

Many ADD individuals battle feelings of anxiety, irritability, and depression. Some have a strong "startle reflex" or they battle panic disorder. Others have heightened sensitivity to sounds or touch. Those who have suffered repeated failures or disappointments from undiagnosed ADD almost always battle low self-esteem and lack of self-confidence. They might want to quit trying. They need reassurance about their worth. This can be a life-crippling syndrome because of ADD.

Many ADDers hyper-focus to achieve success. Then they suffer an emotional letdown afterwards from the strain. Everyone has this experience to a degree for example, when reading or concentrating. But for ADDers, it is much more intense. To "hyper-focus" means to be totally absorbed in some task.

An ADD child or adult may work so hard at focusing on a subject and try to concentrate so intensely, and then become so deeply absorbed in thought while doing it, that it is painful to be jerked away from it. I have had times when I was alone reading or studying, that the sudden interruption of someone walking in and asking me a question felt to me like a bucket of cold water was poured on me. My immediate reaction might be a shocked surprise, like a snake had snuck up under my chair; or sudden anger, leaving me frustrated that my grasp of something or my hold on some idea was now suddenly lost to me.

Long periods of time spent hyper-focusing can be emotionally draining. For ADDers, mood swings are common depending on how alert their brain may be at any time. These mood oscillations ought not to be an excuse. They can be controlled. Here are some non-medical ideas to help keep your moods upbeat and better balanced.

MODERATE MOOD SWINGS

1. *Be aware of your moods.* ADD adults are notoriously poor self-observers, not even noticing when they are tired or hungry or impatient. Have your spouse speak up to help you spot your feelings so you can become more aware of them.

2. *Try deep breathing from your diaphragm.* The Yielded Breath- a prayer of surrender, of peace, of settling your feelings. Take a deep breath in through your nostrils and then let it out slowly through your mouth.

3. *Meditation.* Still your mental storm. Practice listening prayer: "Be still and know that I am God!" It is an ancient practice that is very beneficial.

4. *Physical exercise.* Aerobic emphasis is best. Move your body - calm your mind. Exercise every day! Your heart will love you for it.

5. *Visualization.* Can you picture yourself on a peaceful tropical island? The mind's ability to imagine is powerful and generates real emotions.

6. *Music.* Soothing to the brain, it harmonizes thoughts in a powerful way. Music (the right kind) has power to reinforce good moods or release emotions.

7. *Laughter.* It is a healthy release of pent-up emotions. The Bibles says, "Laughter does good like a medicine." Laughing benefits both body and soul.

8. *A Good Night's Sleep.* This is very important for the body and the brain. Sleep restores brain functionality. Sleep deprivation is epidemic. Any person with ADD absolutely must get sufficient sleep or their symptoms dramatically increase.

9. *Sexual Relations.* Married couples have a bonus! By enjoying frequent and satisfying sexual relationships, the partner with ADD is helped by its many physical and psychological benefits.

ACT TOO QUICKLY?

ADD ADULTS have often been diagnosed with impulsivity. *"Impulsivity is born of a low tolerance for frustration,"* says Susan Roberts, PhD. *"Impulsivity is the tendency to act too quickly and without thinking."*

These impulsive actions are independent of reason. They occur before you think. They are, *"not based on knowing what to do, but doing what you know,"* says Russell Barkley. This characteristic can be moderated by self-discipline or prescribed medication but not ever completely eliminated. Not everyone is designed to think the same way. Some attributes of personality we must live with and indeed, we should celebrate. You are uniquely you!

Quick thoughts; quick feelings; quick actions! Is that you? Do you think faster than you can write? Fluid mental thoughts are often a component of ADD. The ability to channel them and complete the processing of thoughts and images to a conclusion before you lose them is the real challenge, so ADD people try to get it done quickly. I recommend you keep a notepad with you all the time to jot down your ideas.

Anger deserves a further look. It is not harmless when it flares up frequently or is self-directed or destructive. Anger is often a component of ADD yet it is often disguised as some other emotion. With ADDers, anger quickly escalates. It is important to stop anger before it builds. The habit of allowing anger (as a first reaction) should be de-programmed and taken out of our usual behavior. Anger can be kept in check. Unchecked anger, along with impulsivity, can lead to rage and do great harm. My counselor taught me about anger, saying: *"Own your emotions. Anger is what it is. Be honest about it. Don't deny it or stuff it. Deal with it rightly."*

Don't do away with all anger however, since anger is a healthy emotion in mature adults. When it is channeled properly and when it is a response to the appropriate situation, it can save your life or prevent injustice. Even Jesus displayed justifiable anger when he drove the moneychangers from the Temple. Anger, like all human emotions, is a necessary part of life. Emotions make wonderful servants but terrible masters. Keep them under your control.

Knowing these things about ADD is helpful but we also need to face this sad reality—ADD lasts for a lifetime. Deal with it.

Treatment will not make ADD go away. But treatment *"turns down the noise of self-recrimination"* and it reduces the symptoms for many of us. For adults with ADD, treatment is a necessary part of learning to cope. I promise you that your life will get better when you take action. For me, treatment gave me mental focus. Treating yourself will help your whole family. Why? It is vital to understand ADD and how it affects you to understand the dynamics of ADD's impact upon your immediate family.

If you have severe ADD, you should realize that your family is or has been already *negatively* affected. Yes, it has hurt your home. They may feel like they are living with an alcoholic—even if you don't drink! Your loved ones can be **co-dependent** with you because of your ADD condition. Codependency is a syndrome that afflicts families when an adult in the household is an alcoholic. Talk to your doctor or counselor if you suspect this degree of harm has occurred.

To be co-dependent is to be "enmeshed in a dysfunctional relationship." You may be healthy, but you can be affected by a relationship with a family member who is not healthy, whole, or free.

I think one of the best books available on this subject is Melody Beatty's *Codependent No More.* The subtitle is, "How to stop controlling others and start caring for yourself." It is written specifically for adult children of alcoholics—ACOA. In my opinion, that same syndrome can occur in the households that are led by parents who are ADD adults.

PRACTICAL POINTERS

IF YOU KNOW that you have ADD, please take the practical steps I've listed below. Your life—and your family happiness—can be better!

1. *Seek treatment.* Online resources can point you in the right direction. A trained or gifted professional counselor is usually very beneficial and may be a real necessity if you want to improve.

2. *Accept yourself.* If you have a history of failure, realize that there is real hope for you. Your life can change for the better!

3. *Decide to be honest.* Tell trusted people who love you about your issues.

4. *Give intentional gifts of attention to people.* This is an excellent idea! Realize, a lifetime of distraction has taught you bad habits. Your attention

costs you—but with effort you can give it away, especially to those you love.

5. *Practice active listening.* Repeat and clarify. Listen, then ask, "What happened next?" "How did that make you feel?" Slow down your temptation to reply quickly and focus on her or him. Set aside the cell phone. Turn the TV off. Use this "probing question" discussion tool as an aid to effective communication, especially with your spouse. As a husband, I can tell you that she deserves it and she wants it. If you learn how to practice this, the benefits are great.

6. *Make contracts with others.* Put it in writing so you are accountable. Let them tell you the truth!

7. *Structure your life.* Establish a system. Let your spouse know about it. You need a track to run on.

8. *Use reminders.* Use whiteboards, beepers, Day-Timers, smartphone calendars, reminders, or alarms, and sticky notes. Be shameless about this. At work, hire a secretary. In Hebrew Scriptures, a *secretary* is "one who puts in remembrance." Even schedule time for exercise, recreation, or a romantic time with your spouse.

9. *Take breaks.* Admit to yourself and tell others that "Sometimes I need space." Withdraw from too much sensory stimulation. Get centered in your inner core, a place of peace in the eye of the storm. Find inner calmness. Use earplugs or create a quiet room.

For me, I do this with some occasional solitude and with solitary prayer. Take time each day to decompress. Go for a walk, read the Psalms, say your prayers, give thanks, quote your daily affirmations, or listen to soothing music. To do this, find a place of peace and stillness for an extended moment. Make it a priority and a daily habit.

Each week do something that recharges your batteries like going swimming or golfing or walking on the beach or exploring forest trails. Learn to paint or draw. Sit in a quiet place and rest. Eliminate stress from your life even if it restricts your lifestyle. It will be worth it. Stress makes ADD much worse.

Don't forget playtime! Yes, *adult play* is very important. One recreation that I enjoy very much is table tennis (ping pong). I'm good at it. Dr. Daniel Amen has said that table tennis is the very best recreational activity for seniors. Why? It incorporates all the things that we know can help us to have a healthy brain in our mature years. It requires eye-hand coordination, it is low impact, it is aerobic, it makes you move a lot, and it causes your brain to build new neural pathways. Besides all that, it's fun, it is social, and it provokes laughter!

10. *Set boundaries.* Understand and accept your personal limitations. Don't apologize for them. People will like you more and you will like yourself more as well.

TIME MANAGEMENT

AS FOR SCHEDULES, ADDers are unable to set priorities well so they usually need help coping. *First things first!* This is more than just slogan to them; it is something they desperately need to do but truly cannot manage without considerable effort or outside help. Let me emphasize this: when you take time for yourself to organize your life, you are not just serving your own self but you are blessing the people who depend on you. Here are some tools, tips, and Time Management ideas to consider.

Adopt a Daily Routine. Every morning make a list of only three things to do. Rank them in order of importance. Why just three? ADDers are unable to handle long lists or easily prioritize multiple tasks.

Before I knew about ADD, as a young father I watched my children struggle to handle chores or complete tasks. What seemed like laziness or disobedience to me at first, was really their inability to keep track of several things at once or their inability to avoid distractions. If parents could watch out for this, they could train their children more wisely and with more patience.

For adults with ADD, creating good habits can be very beneficial, as habits help us utilize our natural human tendency to do routine things without having to think about them. This works well for me. For example, I am in the habit of laying out my clothes for the next day. I also position particular papers, reminders, or project notes on the top of my desk so they are visible to me when I look for them first thing the next morning. I use visual cues.

Establish Weekly Habits. Choose the same day of each week to do certain tasks. For example, shop for groceries on Saturday. Routinely pay bills on the same day or same date, like the 1st and the 15th. Make the calendar's cyclic routine serve your personal needs so less thought goes into your repetitive tasks. Managing time will always be a difficult, so organize your day the prior evening. Break tasks into small steps. Work in short bursts. And don't forget the Sabbath principle. Take time each week to rest from your work on that set day and to spend quality family time.

Organize your Personal World. Clearing out clutter is quite challenging for us so consider focusing on these three helpful "S" areas: Space, Self, and Stuff.

Space - Everything must be in its place and there must be a place for everything, for example a hook for your car keys. Get into the habit of placing them there. Use files, boxes, and labels. If you don't label it, you will forget what is inside. Use color codes for different stuff. Simplify! Take ten minutes to toss out clutter on a daily basis. This falls under the rule of "pay me now or pay me later," about spending money or spending time. Delay is costly. It will pile up, so deal with it in earlier rather than later before clutter accumulates so much that you can't be efficient.

Self - Reduce reading material, distractions, and visual clutter. A clean desk takes consistent effort but it will bring peace plus greater efficiency. What is in your line of sight? Pull the curtain. What is in your mind? What thoughts are useless? If you can't fix it, dismiss it. What amusement wastes your time? If it is magazines, eliminate them. You'll try to clip and save everything! Keep a clean mind, work at a clean desk, wear clean clothes, and drive a clean car. Bathe yourself daily, mow your yard weekly, and always know how much money is in the checkbook and always know where you children are. Life will be better if you do this.

Make lists before you shop. Don't carry credit cards, checkbook, or too much cash.... you'll forget you spent it and then you may bounce some checks - ugh! Be sure that there is room for laughter in your life every single day. Humor functions like oil in relationships. It reduces friction. And men, do yourself a favor—love your wife. Men who kiss their wife each morning live longer than men who don't. Affection is healthy! You need frequent emotional re-connection, rejuvenation, and rehabilitation.

Stuff - Handle paper only twice: once to scan it, then once again to "FTD" it. This stands for File it, Toss it, or Delegate it. Stacks of paper covering up your desk are a sure sign of ADD or at least, information overload. I only stack papers into piles when I know they are not going to be needed soon, like archives. I know I will instantly forget what's under the top pages of that pile. Like Prego tomato sauce, "It's in there." For me, out of sight literally means out of mind. (Note: your ADD may be different.)

TEND TO YOUR OWN HEALTH

IF YOU LIVE A distracted life, the tendency is to neglect your health. This is a sad reality. You can't love others if you don't first love yourself. You are worth investing care, time, help, and being well. You only get one physical body in this life, so take care of it. Here are some health adjustments, some practical lifestyle areas for you to consider.

DIETARY CHANGES - High Protein-Low Carbohydrate Diet - this is usually a perfect way to eat for ADDers unless your doctor tells you otherwise.

Eat three smaller healthy meals a day plus two lighter snacks between. Five small meals keep you from bottoming out in energy and can help you lose weight. Include protein (lean meats, eggs, nuts, protein powder, cheese, cottage cheese, cream cheese) in your meals. Amino acids are needed for neurotransmitters in the brain to function properly. Use healthy food ideas like more complex carbohydrates in vegetables, rather than white bread, pasta or potatoes. Use oatmeal, whole grain bread or bagels. Watch out for juices and candy. Sugar is not good for ADDers. Reduce or eliminate simple carbohydrates (like white bread, pasta, white rice, potatoes, sugar, corn syrup, honey, candy, and sweet colas). Increase omega-3 fatty acids - tuna, salmon, walnuts, and Brazil nuts. These are "brain foods."

EXERCISE - Essential! Increases blood flow to the brain and raises serotonin levels, which makes you feel good. Exercise five times a week for 30-45 minutes each time. Walk fast to elevate your heart rate, assuming you are healthy enough for vigorous exercise. Here is some good news … a regular sex life with your spouse is very healthy and is genuinely therapeutic for ADDers.

MEDICATION - This is necessary for most but should not be the sole treatment. The most common drugs now are Ritalin, Adderal, Concerta, Focalin, plus other drugs that deal with depression or anxiety. Newer ADD or ADHD drugs might be available. Medication helps the majority - about 75%. Not every prescription will work the same for every person. Work with a physician to find what is best for you and to adjust prescription dosages for the right efficacy.

Also, it is wise to include counseling or coaching as a component of your treatment for ADD. Don't just take a pill without also learning coping skills and disciplines.

COACHING - Have someone to help train you to deal with your disability. They can help you to develop good internal supervision skills. Set personal goals. Learn skills of organizing and planning. They can monitor you for consistent performance and be there to encourage you.

COPING - Get real about you! You need help. Learn to cope. It is a skill. Use visual reminders, practice active listening, and enlist the family or team. Control your environment so you're not overwhelmed by input or to-do lists.

ANTS - Eliminate the "ANTs" - your *Automatic Negative Thoughts*. Dr. Daniel Amen uses this term for critical self-talk and negative mental programming.

Negative self-talk tends toward depression, isolation, and self-hatred. For ANT killers, I recommend a word prescription—the practice of quoting positive Scriptures out loud to yourself. This is in line with telling yourself the truth. It is positive re-programming; healthy for your mind. For example, read Philippians 4:6-8 in the New Testament of the Bible. It is wonderful!

STRUCTURE - ADDers need structure! Organize your space, your self, your stuff, and your time.

Establish priorities after discussions with family or team. Write it down. Hold yourself to it. Place it where you will see it and remember it.

EMOTIONAL TRAUMA - This is very common. Anxiety may be present to the point of Post-Traumatic Stress Syndrome. Deal with it using spiritual, familial, and professional help. Face it, ADD hurts your family relationships. Do something about it. Don't just live with old hurts.

ERRONEOUS BELIEFS - Is your success being sabotaged by repetitive bad habits? Have you failed so often that you now believe the lie that you are a failure? So, you are in debt, again? Divorced, again? Fired, again? Why does this keep happening?

Your beliefs will drive your behavior. Your attitudes will affect your altitude. How much lower can you go? Isn't it time to change the way you think about you and your world? You can change your mind by replacing lies with truth. That exercise is the actual real meaning of the Greek word *metanoia* - repent - in the New Testament.

So, change your beliefs, change your thoughts, change your ways, and thus... change your destiny! Remember this slogan of mine and say it aloud to yourself: *The good news is that the bad news is wrong!*

I specialize in telling people the good news, the truth. That's my job as a minister. Most people are like me in that we don't get it the first time we read it or hear it. Like you, I need reinforcement of what is true. I have to constantly demolish what is false. Based on my experience, I want you to know this: you can change your life!

With God's help, all things are truly possible for you if you will believe the truth. The truth–once you understand it, once you take action based on it–the truth can and will set you free.

What you believe is the basis for your life. It matters. So, think through the beliefs you stand on. They are the foundation stone for your life. Make sure they are tested and true. Don't depend on myths and make-believe.

A CHRISTIAN WITH ADD

FINALLY, FROM A personal perspective, and my experience as a Christian leader, I have some observations from wrestling with this weakness for many decades.

In my struggles, I've learned that God's grace (the divine enabling power that is intended to help us) grows stronger within us only when we acknowledge our weakness.

The key is that I must own my problem first. This power from God is offered to us—present with us— only as we honestly face reality by admitting our need. *"God resists the proud but gives grace to the humble."* So, we need to get real. Don't live in denial. Confess your faults.

Honestly facing our limitations is a form of humility. Our faith can then focus on God's available power, not on our limited human strength. We all need help in different ways.

We are not created equal, at least not in natural abilities. We can't deny our flaws forever nor can we expel a built-in weakness like it was an evil spirit. But we can take our sinful tendencies and habitual weaknesses to the cross to die.

We can learn to cope with our deficiencies and adopt helpful disciplines so that we live in more victory, more peace, and more happiness. By being vulnerable, we can discover community and find love. Don't you want that?

There is true transforming power available to the followers of Christ. The Lord said to the apostle Paul, *"My grace is sufficient for you, for power is perfected in weakness."* (2 Corinthians 12:9) This is an amazing verse. As the Holy Spirit indwells us and as we permit God's word to adjust our way of thinking, we begin to take on more of our heavenly Father's nature thus becoming the very best we can ever be. We can indeed find genuine peace. I know this. It works for me.

What if we conclude that we have ADD? We who are believers in Jesus are not immune to flaws and afflictions just because we know Jesus as our Lord. In fact, Christians ought to be the ultimate realists, facing the human situation with no illusions. Sin is real and evil is real and we are powerless to save ourselves.

Therefore, we need the Savior! Jesus proved His love for us when He died on the cross to redeem us from our sins and bring us to God. He proved His power to save us when He rose from the dead with eternal life as a gift for everyone who chooses Him. (John 1:12)

As a Christian, with all of this help available to me, I have no excuse for staying angry or frustrated or depressed or impatient. By faith, I can tap into God's available grace. I choose God based on His love, not due to a religious guilt trip.

Yes—I have ADD. No—I won't use it to justify bad behavior. I will not say, "But that's just the way I am!" Instead, I will rely on God for help. I will repent of self-deception. I will confess my flaws. I will walk in the truth. I will grow. I will trust others. I will say "Yes!" to what God's word says about me. I will believe what it says about Him. I will keep on repenting, believing, and loving. I will ask for help, repeatedly. I will adapt and grow as a (being daily redeemed) human being.

I can take the practical steps of making lifestyle choices to moderate my weakness. I will purposefully tend to my spiritual needs. For example, I worship God with the Holy Spirit's help every day, sometimes several times a day.

I know from my own life that any time spent in prayer—in quiet adoration of the Lord, in respecting His presence and contemplating His thoughts in the

Scriptures, by softly singing praises or Scripture choruses within my heart—is as soothing to my mind as oil poured out on the top of troubled water.

Worship or meditation has a delightful, lingering, peaceful effect on my soul for hours afterward. And peace is something us ADDers need more of.

I have learned this also in my life. ADD gives me a unique and vibrant walk with the Lord. It gives me an extra spiritual sensitivity. I absorb what I read from the Bible quickly. I can pick up clues, discern things others miss, see connections. I can hear the gentle voice of the Lord when I get still and calm my soul by spending time waiting on Him. I could give you many examples of this happening. It is an asset in my role of serving the church as a spiritual person.

Look at it this way: We ADDers are gifted with a weakness that compels us to lean on God for the help we need; to consciously draw on the Lord's grace. Irresponsible behavior or holding on to a bad attitude has no acceptable excuse. The Bible has no "exception clause" in the list of the fruit of the Spirit (Galatians 6) that would exempt ADDers from showing Christian character such as patience, gentleness, forbearance, self-control, etc. These things are not easy for ADDers!

Christians have an advantage here. We who follow Jesus and believe the Bible can rely on God's word rather than just on our changeable feelings.

Telling the truth to our self is an important part of becoming whole. We learn the truth from how life works and from the Bible, which says that we are uniquely loved and valued for who we are despite our weaknesses or handicaps. Indeed, our heavenly Father is delighted to show mercy to us in our daily struggles, giving us power to overcome.

Make your own ADD a matter of personal prayer. Having a disability is real but it does not justify sinning or harming others. If you feel powerless, then you are qualified - you're a candidate for grace to help.

If you think you might have ADD, my informed but by no means professional advice is this: don't jump to conclusions. Don't medically diagnose yourself. *Don't* start using ADD as an excuse for irresponsibility. *Do* talk it over with your spouse, a trusted pastor, or a qualified health care provider. Read more on the subject so you can be armed with good information. Pray and ask God to help you truly and honestly know yourself.

Forgive yourself for failing, laugh at yourself for your foibles, enjoy being you, and focus on developing and utilizing your strengths. Don't try to eradicate all your weaknesses. You'll only wear yourself out trying. You can't, anyway.

If you conclude that you likely do have ADD, try to honestly evaluate its affect upon yourself and those around you. Talk it over with someone you trust. Consider obtaining professional counseling by someone who specializes in this disorder to help you deal with the emotional damage you may have suffered or inflicted on others. It is highly likely that you have been adversely affected in your work, in your education, and in your marriage. Don't limp through life—get well!

I hope that you consult with a qualified medical provider who is knowledgeable about treatments for ADD. Your physician, along with your counselor, can be a true source of solid assistance to help you become the person you were meant to be.

As you learn to handle ADD in your family, let me know how it goes. I would love to hear from you. Your comments would be appreciated and may help to benefit others.

RECOMMENDED READING

IF THIS BOOKLET is helpful to you, buy more copies to give away to family or friends. You can order my paperback books from Amazon.com or other retailers.

As you'll see in my byline, I write for love not for money. Income from book sales allows me work at what I love: I love helping people. I write newspaper columns, online articles, and Youtube videos.

I've been writing about faith, family, country, and church for decades and I've been fortunate to have hundreds of articles published. No single article provoked as much response as did my column on ADD.

I believe you can arm yourself with truth. I hope I've helped you to be better informed. You can absorb practical information from folks who share their own life story.

You saw that I have quoted freely from some great writers. In fact, I lost track of many exact references - proving that I have ADD! There is no intentional plagiarism; just me being me. I have referenced every written source I learned from in the Bibliography, although not the precise page numbers.

These authors were my initial primary guides as I began to desperately search so I could understand myself better. They helped me greatly. Their thoughts are mixed into my own ideas. I am grateful for them. You can obtain their books at your local bookstore or perhaps your favorite on-line bookseller. Check out these resources and see more in my bibliography.

BIBLIOGRAPHY

1. **Think Fast - The A.D.D. Experience** by Tom Hartmann and Janie Bowman. An excellent book incorporating good ideas - very helpful.

2. **Living with A.D.D. - A Workbook for Adults** by Susan Roberts. Practical. (with Dr. Ratep's comments)

3. **Attention Deficit Disorder - A Different Perspective** by Tom Hartmann. A valuable resource.

4. **Healing A.D.D.** by Daniel Amen, M.D. Dr. Amen has done extensive original medical research with brain scans showing real physiological brain images common to those with ADD.

5. **Adult A.D.D.** by Thomas Whiteman and Michelle Novotini. My favorite if I had only one book.

6. **Honey Are You Listening?** By Rick Fowler, M.D. and Jerilyn Fowler. My wife's favorite! We read it first many years ago. I remember how very helpful it was to us as a married couple. Includes a diagnostic quiz.

7. **A.D.D. - Wandering Minds and Wired Bodies** a small booklet by Edward T. Welch. For Christian parents with ADD kids.

8. **Driven to Distraction** and **Married to Distraction** by Edward Hallowell.

9. **Delivered from Distraction** by Hallowell and John Ratey.

10. **Finding Your Focus** by Judith Greenbaum.

11. **The Gift of Adult A.D.D.** by Lara Honos-Webb.

12. **Ten Simple Solutions to A.D.D.** by Stephen Moulton Sarkins.

ACKNOWLEDGEMENTS

MY HEARTFELT THANKS to my lovely wife, Lana! She knows first-hand the trials of living with ADD in her family. Lana is a real champion to me, a straight-line thinker; my perfect and lovely friend; and my ministry partner for these many years. We are a very happy couple, a true team. Besides assisting churches in Arkansas and ministry teams in the USA, we supply Bible training materials and charitable aid to emerging church leaders in developing nations through Touched By Grace Inc., our 501-c-3, a non-profit religious corporation founded in 1998. You can learn more at www.touchedbygrace.org.

I wish to thank Dr. Michael Nanney, M.D., with Primary Care Associates, who was my personal physician in Mississippi. He kindly read this manuscript and wrote a foreword. He is a knowledgeable physician and a brother in Christ. I recommend him.

Special thanks to Dr. Daniel Patterson, M.D., in Wilmington, North Carolina (retired). I was fortunate to find him and very glad that he could take me as a patient in his busy practice since he was also a Forensic Psychiatrist. It was Dr. Patterson who encouraged me to write this book. His advice meant a great deal to me and gave me hope. He was the physician who first confirmed my ADD and began my treatment. He helped me apply real science, good understanding, coping skills, family counseling, and for a season, the use of medications he prescribed. I am grateful for his professional skill and the gratifying friendship we developed. His valuable comments also are included in the Foreword. He has since retired from his practice.

ABOUT THE AUTHOR

RON WOOD is a husband, father, and grandfather, and he has Adult ADD. He is a writer, minister, and teacher. He is the author of several books. He graduated from Bible College (Southeastern University) in Lakeland, Florida, where he earned a degree in Missions. Ron is a scholar in God's word. He began reading the Bible and experiencing spiritual gifts when he was young. He is associated with Network Ecclesia International. He worked his way through college as a reporter for an NBC radio station. He has hundreds of newspaper columns published.

Ron and his wife, Lana, met as freshmen at college and studied Missions and Bible to prepare for ministry. In 2001, they lived in South Africa as missionaries. Ron and Lana have served various churches for 45 years in the southeastern United

States (Southern Baptist, Assembly of God, Freewill Baptist, and Non-Denominational).

Ron upholds the Bible as the word of God and serves the whole body of Christ. He is known for his prophetic insight and his humor when he teaches or ministers at churches, conferences, or seminars. Ron has hosted call-in talk-radio shows, recorded broadcasts for podcasts, and produced a radio show, *The Father's Power*. Many articles are posted at the website, www.touchedbygrace.org.

In his teachings, Ron applies years of Bible study and personal experiences ministering the gifts of the Spirit. His books are available at Amazon.com.

Ron and Lana live in Arkansas where they enjoy being close to their two adult children, Scott and Rebekah, and their six lovely and brilliant grandchildren.

Damaged by Adult ADD is available at Amazon.com and other online book retailers.

Made in the USA
Columbia, SC
01 June 2021